Meeting the Challenge

DEALING WITH CRACK AND COCAINE ADDICTION

A workbook for use by individuals in one-to-one or group work sessions

Written and compiled by Valerie Peets

DrugScope

DrugScope

Meeting the Challenge
dealing with crack and cocaine addiction

Published by
DrugScope
Suite 204
2nd Floor
Prince Consort House
109-111 Farringdon Road
London EC1R 3BW
Telephone: 020 7520 7555
E-mail: info@drugscope.org.uk
Website: www.drugscope.org.uk

First published 2004

© DrugScope 2004. All rights reserved. No portion of this publication may be reproduced, stored or transmitted in any format whatsoever without the express permission of the publisher.

ISBN 190431 9211

Design: Andrew Haig Associates

Printed by: RAP

Acknowledgments
Most of the content in this booklet has been redesigned and updated from previously existing material. We are unable to credit any specific source but we will be happy to do so in future reprints if you contact us with the details.

CONTENTS

Personal development programme	2
A fun quiz to test your knowledge	3
The facts about "crack"	5
Health	11
Tips for giving up	13
Crack cocaine using cycle	15
Overdose	16
Cocaine and alcohol	17
Triggers and cravings	18
The decision	20
Why do you do it?	26
The heebie-jeebies	28
Lack of sleep	29
Relapse	32
Cravings	35
My plan to change	37
Staying clean	43
Appendix A: Personal "Self Plan"	45
Appendix B: Certificate	46
Crack cocaine quiz answers	47

DRUG AWARENESS

PERSONAL DEVELOPMENT PROGRAMME
"Meeting The Challenge"
dealing with crack and cocaine addiction

NAME _____

Date	Sections of workbook/ pages covered	Issues raised which need further discussion	Comments
1	Welcome – Ground rules		
2			
3			
4			
5			
6	Where do I go from here? Presentation of certificate		

To Start

A Fun Quiz To Test Your Knowledge

CRACK AND COCAINE HEALTH QUIZ

Answer each question, TRUE or FALSE

(answers on p47)

- It is okay to use crack/cocaine if you have a bad heart. It helps your heart by making it beat faster.

    TRUE/FALSE

- Damage to the brain by smoking crack/cocaine is mainly caused by what is generally known as a stroke.

    TRUE/FALSE

- Crack lung is caused by smoking in badly ventilated crack houses.

    TRUE/FALSE

- There is no increased risk of catching TB through smoking crack/cocaine.

    TRUE/FALSE

- Crack/cocaine users are prone to skin complaints.

    TRUE/FALSE

- If someone is schizophrenic they can help their condition by using crack/cocaine.

    TRUE/FALSE

- Crack/cocaine use can cause dehydration, headaches, kidney damage, physical and mental fatigue, stress, anxiety, muscle pains and insomnia.

    TRUE/FALSE

- There is no risk of catching HIV or hep C from using crack/cocaine.

    TRUE/FALSE

- Doctors have a duty to report crack/cocaine use to the Home Office if you tell them about it.

    TRUE/FALSE

- The feeling of insects crawling under your skin "coke bug" is caused by the crack/cocaine reacting with your shower gel on your skin.

    TRUE/FALSE

- You can't overdose on crack/cocaine unless you inject it.

    TRUE/FALSE

THE FACTS ABOUT "CRACK"

Crack and Cocaine

How it works

Crack and cocaine are not physically addictive, BUT they can create very strong feelings and sensations which feel like physical addiction.

Crack and cocaine work by stimulating the release of body chemicals which govern our instinctive responses to danger and reward/reinforce behaviour.

The increased levels of one of these chemicals adrenaline, make you more aware and the others, dopamine and serotonin, make you feel high.

Dopamine and serotonin play an important role in our mental and physical health. The specialised cells containing them are situated in the mid brain area.

Cocaine stimulates the release of the dopamine, but prevents its re-uptake, which in turn leads to its depletion or reduction. This increases the high, but ultimately leads to what is called the crash.

| Hit of crack or cocaine | ➡ | Dopamine gives initial high, reinforces a learnt process and develops anticipation or want for drug | ➡ | Serotonin gives repeated pleasure and prolonged highs |

Separate research is also suggesting that crack and cocaine can cause temporary damage to the part of the brain that is responsible for inhibiting bad behaviour and rational decision-making.

CRAVING ➡ Release of adrenaline triggered by money, places etc.

Dopamine reinforces learnt behaviour and adds to anticipation.

Rational thinking processes are poor and the brain's inhibitors are not working.

USE ➡

Adrenaline

Danger response
Fight or Flight

Adrenaline heightens the senses and enables the body to work at peak performance.

Released because of a cue trigger such as money, people, area, or day of the week etc. and thereafter by each intake of crack or cocaine.

Heart rate increases: increases the blood flow around the body, which also increases the speed at which oxygen gets to the muscles.

Breathing rate increases: short, shallow breaths increase the amount of oxygen in the bloodstream.

Butterflies: due to oxygen leaving the stomach and being sent to the arms and legs where it is most needed.

Sweating: the body thinking that it will get hotter by either fighting or fleeing starts the cooling down system.

Shaking: due to the increased energy in the body. Muscles are ready to go into action.

The list above is how most people describe cravings.

Prolonged release of adrenaline produces:

- Less need for sleep
- Loss of appetite
- Visual & auditory hallucinations
- Impaired ability to think about and control actions
- Severe anxiety
- Paranoia

The increased paranoia is due to the brain trying to make sense of the danger response of "fight" or "flight".

Dopamine & Serotonin

Reward and reinforcement of behaviour
Dopamine and serotonin are chemicals in the brain which are responsible for rewarding and reinforcing behaviour and for balancing moods. They make us feel good and their release into our system is calibrated on a kind of scale.

High release SEX	The more sex, the more babies, the more babies, the more chance of the human race surviving. Orgasm is the feeling of reward.
Medium release SOCIAL CONTACT	To help us work together, form communities, makes us stronger and increases survival chances.
Low release FOOD	We need to eat to stay alive and healthy. This increases our chances of survival and of those depending on us.

Crack and cocaine use causes the release of dopamine and serotonin in larger quantities than normal.

This puts crack and cocaine use way above sex in the reward and reinforcement scale.

This leads the brain to believe that this is one of the most important actions regarding human survival.

This in turn contributes to the compulsive nature of cocaine.

Dopamine and Serotonin depletion (reduction)

Crack and cocaine use not only provokes the release of dopamine and serotonin, but it also prevents their re-uptake once they are released. This causes the "come down" or "crash" which makes the user feel bad and reinforces the need for another hit, then another, then another, then another............

> *In simple terms, what happens is this, when we do something that is pleasurable, chemicals are released into our brain which make us feel good and so reinforce the behaviour which caused the good feeling. This makes us want to repeat the behaviour. In normal circumstances this is fine because the chemicals released are reabsorbed back into the system, so we can repeat the behaviour without any ill effects.*

> *The problem arises when these chemicals are released because of stimulant use. The action of the drugs on the brain stops the chemicals from being reabsorbed, thus leading to a reduction of these "feel good" chemicals within the brain. This leads to the feelings of needing to use to feel better, but the more use, the bigger the crash because of the lack of chemicals in the brain.*

> *In other words, the more used, the more the need to use.*

That is why the depletion of these chemicals causes a very strong clinical depression which added to depression caused by adverse circumstances, such as losing one's job, partner etc., can lead to suicidal tendencies. Dopamine and serotonin depletion also brings on mood swings and users generally aren't interested in any activity that isn't associated with the use of crack and cocaine.

It takes approximately six to eight weeks in normal circumstances, and without using drugs, for these chemicals to be replaced.

HEALTH

Crack use has serious effects on health

The effects already outlined, depression, paranoia, anxiety, confusion, difficulty sleeping, difficulty relaxing, are mainly due to the effects of the drug on the brain.

Other problems include, loss of weight, and general poor health due to scarce or bad eating, and to the effect that the drug has on the immune system.

More serious side effects are risks of heart failure, brain damage and the risk of strokes, damage to the liver, to the respiratory system and the kidneys, stomach ulcers, and skin problems. Crack and cocaine can lead to increased severity of attacks of sickle cell and can lead to epilepsy because medication becomes ineffective.

Pregnancy
Crack and cocaine use is not advisable during pregnancy as any substance at this time could have an adverse effect. Using at this time **may** cause,

> Spontaneous abortion; because the placenta detach itself from the womb;
>
> Babies born underweight, due to the lack of nourishment;
>
> Disturbed behaviour in newborn babies, due to high adrenaline levels.

Psychiatric issues
There are a lot of things which effect mental health, these can be due to chemical imbalances in the brain and also to social/environmental factors.

Because of the effect that crack and cocaine have on the brain it is very important that users who have contact with the psychiatric services inform them of their drug use, otherwise mis-diagnosis can occur.

> Depression can be caused by depletion/reduction of dopamine and serotonin and also by life's events brought about by chronic drug use. Some drugs used to treat depression, such as Prozac, work by promoting

the release of serotonin. If there is little serotonin to release, these drugs can be ineffective. Therefore it is important that crack users, who visit a doctor for depression, tell the doctor about their use.

Other psychiatric complications that have been associated with crack and cocaine include

- Drug induced psychosis
- Attention Deficit Hyperactivity Disorder
- Paranoia
- Anxiety disorders
- Repetitive disorders

Hepatitis – HIV – TB

Crack cocaine users are at risk from infections such as hepatitis C, hepatitis B and HIV.

These can be caught when blood is passed from person to person as a result of cuts and burns around the mouth and lips, for instance from using tin cans. It is best to use always your own pipe or tube, don't share. If you or your friends have dried or cracked lips the risk of infection increases, so use lip balm or Vaseline and drink plenty of water, which will keep you hydrated and help to prevent cracked lips.

There is increasing concern that crack users may be at risk from airborne viruses, including TB, due to using the drug in houses and flats that have poor ventilation.

Many infections are spread sexually. Always use condoms. Some infections are spread by oral sex and having cuts and sores around the mouth. Using condoms for oral sex helps to protect you.

TIPS FOR GIVING UP

If you're thinking of stopping using, then the same applies as for any other drug – avoid the triggers as far as possible.

Decide
Make up your mind that this is what you want to do and gather some support from drug workers, family, non-using friends etc.

Triggers
Work out what triggers your using, e.g., friends, places etc. and avoid them as far as possible.

Plan
Plan to give up, "just for today". Plan your time to minimise the boredom and time to kill which is the biggest cause of relapse. Establish a daily routine, such as exercise. This stimulates natural endorphins (chemicals) which in turn help to lift your mood and make you feel better. Recognise the danger time of day when you might be using and keep busy. Look for new activities, voluntary work, support groups, college etc.

Support
Stopping using will mean that you will feel pretty rough for a while and could mean that you are going to feel very down. This is where the support of family and non-using friends comes in, but if things are really bad, see your doctor.

Clear out
Get rid of anything you have which relates to drug use, e.g., foil, and old pipes, take dealer's phone numbers off your phone.

Money
Don't carry a lot of money or credit cards. Limit the amount that you carry to less than £10 for the time being. Too much money starts cravings, so carry stamped envelopes, post them to yourself, you'll get the money in the morning and in the meantime will have had time to think.

Health
Take care of yourself, eat nutritious meals and take exercise. Be kind to yourself.

Thinking
When you start to think about using, try to switch your thinking to something else. Remember why you decided to stop.

Time
Find other ways to fill your time to avoid sitting around thinking of using.

Acupuncture
Auricular (in the ear) acupuncture or massage can help with craving and help you relax.

Remember – The longer you wait to give up the more of your life you will waste, BUT – if at first you don't succeed, try again! A lapse needn't turn into a full-blown relapse.

The longer you stay away from crack the easier it becomes.

Reward

Treat yourself with something non-drug related for staying away from crack.

CRACK COCAINE USING CYCLE

The mission

High cravings triggered by cues such as people, places, money etc.

Adrenaline released and urges to use reinforced by dopamine, increasing the anticipation.

If long term use then behaviour inhibitors affected which can lead to elaborate justifications and irrational behaviour in order to score.

Drug Use

Initial quick high achieved, though is for a short time. Beginning crash reinforces the compulsion to use again, but same highs cannot be reached due to nervous system trying to maintain a balance.

Increased levels of adrenaline leading to lack of sleep/appetite, anxiety and paranoia.

Recovery

Some of the feelings of the crash have worn off. Users may have slept and eaten food.

Feelings of depression (can reinforce using again) may still be strong, depending on whether a daily or bingeing pattern is being followed.

User feels more in control, physically better and is now open to the cue triggers again.

Comedown crash

Session has finished or drugs have run out.

High levels of adrenaline leading to the feeling of being "prang" or "wired".

Depressant drugs used to try and level things out and lessen the feelings.

High levels of remorse and chemically-induced depression.

OVERDOSE

It is easy to use too much crack cocaine and overdose (particularly if you inject)

Crack increases the heart rate but closes down the blood vessels. This results in increased blood pressure and heat building up inside the body which can't escape.

The first signs of overdose can include a sudden rise in body temperature, a flushed face, hot skin but no sweating and muscle cramps or stiffness in the arms and legs.

If this happens it's important to cool the person down by loosening clothing and putting cold, wet towels on their head and neck. If there's any ice to hand, rub it around their neck. Don't give anything to eat or drink except sips of cold water.

COCAINE & ALCOHOL

Cocaine and alcohol are a potentially lethal mixture. Research has shown that taken together they produce a chemical called "cocaethylene." This chemical has a longer duration of action in the brain and is more toxic than either drug alone.

TRIGGERS AND CRAVINGS

Commit crime to support crack habit. Shoplifting CDs from record shop

⬇

Crime releases adrenaline, adds to craving and gives £££££££

⬇

Use crack and end up bingeing until run out of money

⬇ ⬆

Don't go near record shops. Look at cycle of using

Open cravings

Full on cravings with no justification, just want to use. Cravings in between pipes etc.

Hidden cravings

Lots of justification or unconscious ploys used to get into a using situation. This becomes more common when trying to stop.

Misinterpreted cravings

Situations that produce a natural release of adrenaline, or build up of stress, e.g. interviews, threats, dentists etc.

This book does not aim to be the definitive guide to giving up
Its motto is,

"If at first you don't succeed, try again, and again and again"

The basic principles of which are:
Make the decision
Gather support
Plan strategies
Decide on your goals

HAVE A GO

ADDICTION IS A CHOICE
It's *your* choice

THE DECISION

The first step, making the decision

It's *your* choice! Yes, that's right, ADDICTION IS A CHOICE

You are responsible for your own actions, if you want to give up, it's up to you, no one can make that decision for you.

You choose

It's your decision

The first step towards giving up is actually making the decision that this is really what you want to do.

No, not your partner, mother, kids, uncle Tom Cobbley and all, but you!

It's okay to want to give up because of your partner, family etc., but the more reasons that you have for doing it for yourself, the more chance you have of succeeding and making it through the bad times.

So, let's look at some of the REASONS

Reasons I started using	Reasons I do it now

Now look at your list and see which:

- Are a result of your drug use
- Will still be around when you come off
- You can't do anything about
- You can do something about
- Are your responsibility
- Aren't your responsibility

This isn't to make you feel guilty or to find someone to blame, but to help you understand your situation, so that you can start to find ways to sort things out.

We are not responsible for some of the things that happen to us, like the old adage says, "Shit happens!" It's how we respond to these situations, which shapes our lives. It's up to you whether or not drugs are part of your response or if you find and use other coping mechanisms.

If you feel that you can make that decision for yourself, because it's what you want to do, then let's look at some strategies that might help you...

One step at a time!

Why should you give up?

Lets look at the pros and cons,

taking drugs		not taking drugs	
Benefits	**Costs**	**Benefits**	**Costs**
getting high	upsetting partner, family	better relationships	what to do about drug using friends
feeling good	affecting children	more time for kids	won't have a way to relax
	costing too much money	better health	too much time on my hands
	grafting to support habit	not committing crime/no fear of arrest	
	damaging health	more money to spend	
	committing crime/risk of imprisonment		

These are just a few of the reasons for and against giving up. Think about your own reasons for wanting to give up and for using. Write them all down using the blank form on the next page.

Fill in the blank form with your own reasons and see what you come up with

taking drugs		not taking drugs	
Benefits	Costs	Benefits	Costs

Understanding what you are doing and why you are doing it is the first step towards dealing with the problem.

Where are you?

The cycle of change

This "Cycle" can be used to help modify any unwanted behaviour. For instance, eating too much, drinking, smoking, drug taking. Study the diagram and work out where you think you are. If you've just got this book, you're probably in "Contemplation" or "Action," but could just as easily be anywhere else on the circle.

Most people go around the circle a few times before finally managing to give up.

THE CYCLE OF CHANGE

CONTEMPLATION
– see behaviour as problematic and begin to weigh up pros and cons of changing

DECISION
- to change or continue as before

PRECONTEMPLATION
– individual sees no problem, others do

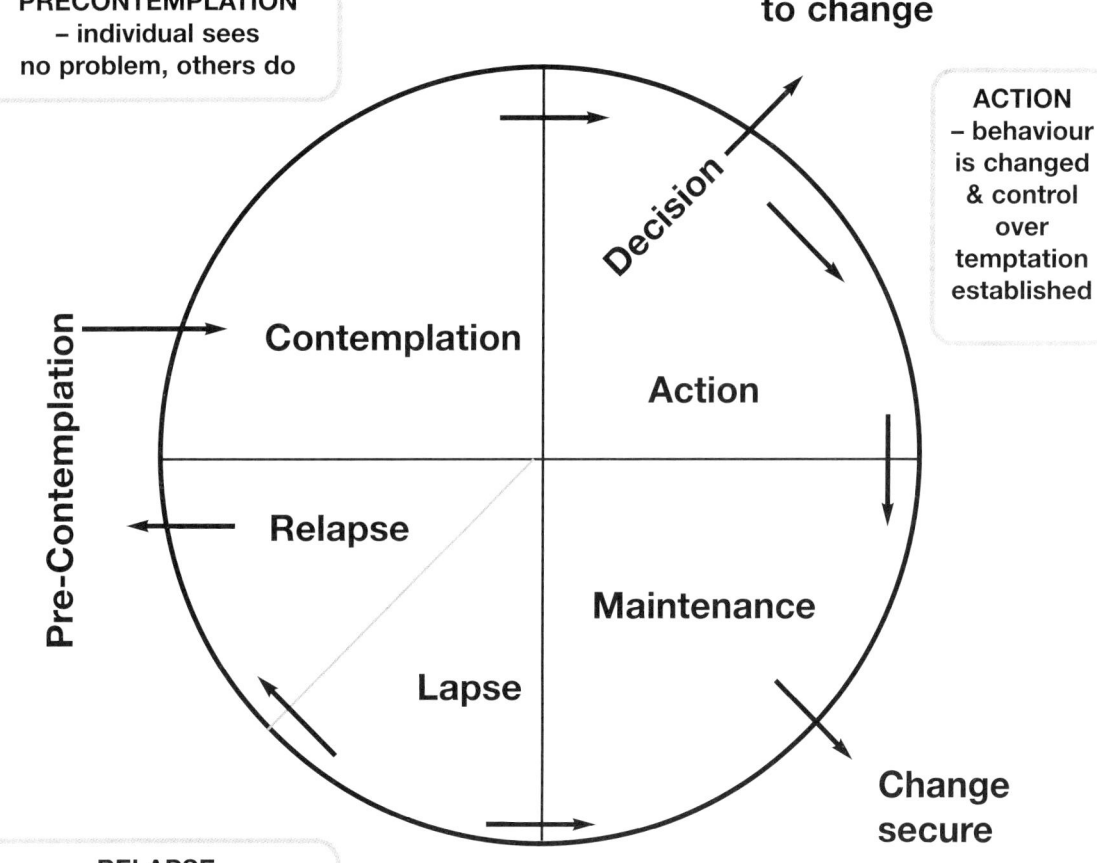

Choose not to change

ACTION
– behaviour is changed & control over temptation established

Cycle diagram: Pre-Contemplation → Contemplation → Decision → Action → Maintenance → Change secure; with Lapse and Relapse returning toward Pre-Contemplation/Contemplation.

Change secure

RELAPSE
– may lapse and return to previous pattern of behaviour

LAPSE
– making changes does not guarantee that a minor slip or lapse will not occur

MAINTENANCE
- continuing to act in accordance with the change which now becomes part of the established behaviour

WHY DO YOU DO IT?

Drug use diary

Try keeping a diary for a few days. Look at the who, when, where and why of your using. Be honest, because at the end of the day, you'll only be kidding yourself. This will enable you to analyse some of the things for yourself so that you can think about avoiding some of the triggers to your using.

A suggested format is this:

Date:

- **What time of day was it when you felt like using?**
- **If you did use, how much did you use?**
- **How did you use the substance? (e.g. injecting, smoking, etc)**
- **Did you use alone, or with other people?**
- **How did you feel just before you used? (e.g. happy, lonely, agitated, tired, bored, stressed out, etc.)**
- **How did you feel just after you had used?**
- **How long did this feeling last?**
- **How did you feel once the effects of using had worn off?**
- **Then write down any other comments or thoughts you may have**

Once you've written up your diary for a few days in a row, you may be able to see a pattern emerging. Use this as a blueprint to help yourself. Look at it carefully to see if there are any obvious situations, people etc., to avoid. It won't be easy, but you need to start somewhere.

It's all about thinking about and adopting strategies that work for you. Everybody is different, what works for one doesn't work for another.

Avoid the people you use with, will you really have the strength to give up while all around you are using?

If boredom is one of the main reasons for your using, put strategies in place to avoid boredom. What interests you? It could be anything from a walk in the park to voluntary work. "No money" is not an excuse. Jogging is free, if that's too radical, so are libraries.

Which brings me to one of the main triggers, "GIRO DAY," "PAY DAY." This is a tough one! Some people, well on their way to controlling their habit, still find it impossible not to score on giro/pay day. But you can still cut down.

Don't carry a lot of money, bank or credit cards. Limit the amount that you carry to less than £10 for the time being. Too much money starts cravings, so carry stamped envelopes, post them to yourself, you'll get the money in the morning and in the meantime will have had time to think.

Avoid situations where you know you will be tempted to use. This all comes back to your own motivation and to being honest with yourself.

One of the main things to remember is that by the time most people come to the stage that they feel they want to give up, they have been using for some time. Be patient, be kind to yourself. Remember one step at a time, you won't put right in a few days what took you a long time to mess up.

Above all, be honest with the people who are supporting you. They can only help if they know what the bottom line is. You may not want to tell your mum the whole truth, but please be open with your doctor and drug worker. It's no good telling them that you're using only one rock a day if you're on five. It's like going to the doctor and telling him that you've a broken arm, when you've really got a broken leg. With the best will in the world, he'll treat the broken arm, but you'll be no better off, because you'll still be limping when you leave the surgery.

The moral is, be honest with your workers, you're not going to shock them, they are not going to judge you, they've heard it all before. They have your best interests at heart and wouldn't be doing the job if they didn't want to help.

THE HEEBIE-JEEBIES

Or whatever else you want to call it

Most people who use drugs didn't just wake up one morning and decide that they would become addicted. They've usually travelled a long rocky road before they get to the point where they are contemplating giving up.

Some have suffered tragedy and loss and used drugs as a way of dealing with these. Others are so disillusioned, lacking in self-esteem and unable to deal with the ups and downs of life, that drugs are their comforter, their way of coping.

There are as many different reasons for drug use as there are drug users. But one thing that does happen to many is that once they start to become "clean", they are forced to deal with all the problems that the drugs have been masking.

This is where the support network really comes in. If you have access to counselling that's great, if not, find someone you can trust and talk to. Your doctor, drug worker, a close friend or an understanding relative, can help you develop other strategies as ways of coping.

Remember you've probably been "out of it" for quite a while, so it will take time for your body and brain to return to anything like normality. All the thoughts and feelings that you have been covering up will surface with a vengeance. The little devils will try to catch you when you are at your most vulnerable and really work a number on you if you let them. This is one of the phases that need to be worked through on the way.

Look at it in a positive way: you are one step nearer to your goal. It's as if you're in training; all that muscle aching that needs to be endured before getting fit. If this is happening to you, you must be getting somewhere!

LACK OF SLEEP

As if the Heebie – Jeebies aren't enough, it's now impossible to sleep!

This is another problem that you will encounter as you try to give up.

We develop a natural sleep pattern in response to day and night, but the use of drink and drugs can override this system, so that when you stop using, your body has forgotten how to go to sleep and has to relearn.

Relying on alcohol and drugs to get off to sleep sends your body's natural pattern haywire and you lose your natural ability to get to sleep. Also, using depressants like alcohol or "Benzos" may knock you out but you may not sleep deeply or feel properly rested the next day. People who rely on drugs to get to sleep often wake up in the middle of the night when the effects wear off and then take something else to get back to sleep.

Not being able to sleep is one of the main reasons that makes people lapse back into drug use.

If you really want to give up be prepared to deal with poor sleep.

SELF HELP TIPS – TO TAKE YOU THROUGH THE NIGHT

- Set a pattern – try to go to bed and get up at the same time each day.

- Force yourself to get up in the morning and be active during the day.

- Don't nap – try not to sleep during the day.

- Avoid stimulants – cut down on tea, coffee, fizzy drinks, alcohol and smoking at least 2 hours before going to bed.

- Don't eat or drink late in the evening.

- Make sure the bedroom is comfortable – not too hot or cold, not stuffy.

- Try to stay awake doing mental arithmetic or reading a book.

- Count to yourself – try counting backwards from 1000 and picture each number in your mind.

- If you can't get to sleep get up and do something else to relax like watching TV or reading a book. Go back to bed when you feel sleepy.

- Problems always seem much worse in the middle of the night. If you wake up worrying about problems, write them down to clear your head and think about them in the morning.

LET'S EXPLODE SOME MYTHS ABOUT SLEEP

People always get enough sleep to survive; it's just that it doesn't always feel like it

- **People need an average of eight hours sleep per night**

    FALSE

    Different people need different amounts of sleep. Some manage well on 5 hours, others need 10.

- **Regular exercise helps to overcome sleep problems**

    TRUE

    Exercise does help sleep problems.

- **As you get older you need more sleep**

    FALSE

    The older you get the less sleep you need.

- **If I don't get enough sleep I will become ill**

    FALSE

    Our bodies take as much sleep as they need. Lack of sleep may make us feel uncomfortable, but only in very extreme cases will it make us ill.

- **If you don't get to sleep in 30 minutes you should give up and take a sleeping tablet**

    FALSE

    The use of sleeping tablets will only mask any bad sleeping habits you might develop.

RELAPSE

Triggers

What causes relapse?

Giving up any addiction is not easy. You may have to avoid some triggers for the rest of your life.

It is important that you identify your own triggers, so that you can avoid some and be prepared for others. This way you can work out how to deal with them and take control of the situation. Some things are common to all users, but some are more individual. One man stopped going to the chip shop when he realised that the smell of vinegar was his trigger.

Think about what causes relapse, add your triggers to the list,

What causes relapse?

boredom	loneliness	no money
peer pressure	complacency	having money

Or, just about anything you can think of

the media	poverty	the government
music	feeling good	feeling bad

Some others might include:

| arguments | £10 notes | silver foil |

Being aware of your triggers is the best way to cope with them, but don't get complacent or try to test yourself. Don't expose yourself to unnecessary risk, people or situations.

Each time that you cope with a trigger it will give you confidence and it may be easier the next time.

KEEPING IT UP – IS NOT EASY!

It involves lots of things, some of which are:

- **Avoiding triggers** – identify your own, look at some strategies to help yourself.

- **Change in environment** – there are drugs everywhere, you can't move away from them. But you may decide a change of place is for the best, or just avoid people who you know will be using, or places where you know you can score.

- **Incentive, rewards, rules, planning** – set small achievable goals, reward yourself with something non-drug related when you achieve them.

- **On going support** – make use of support networks.

- **Walk before you run** – take one step at a time.

- **Time management** – plan your days so that you don't have time to think about using. Plan activities, keep busy.

- **Avoiding complacency** – don't become complacent.

- **Being realistic** – be realistic in your expectations. Things are not going to be easy just because you've given up drugs.

- **Regular reassessment of goals** – as you progress reset your goals to keep moving forward positively.

- **Honesty** – be honest with yourself and others. There will be times when you feel down, or things are difficult and you need extra support.

- **Maintaining self-esteem, dignity** – look after yourself, be kind to yourself.

- **Courage** – you knew that it wasn't going to be easy. Believe in yourself, you can do it.

CRAVINGS

Most people experience cravings...

Cravings can vary in intensity from ...

"Fleeting feelings"

To

"Pacing around for hours totally dominated by thoughts and feelings about the drug"

People report craving for a long time after stopping

BUT

These cravings are not very intense and they tend to happen very infrequently

People often hear stories of never ending cravings

This can lead to despondency, so it is important to get craving into perspective

They will become less frequent and less intense over time

"Cravings seem to last forever"

By examining cravings you may find that they only last for a few minutes. The feeling will rise, peak and then fall.

FOUR TYPES OF CRAVINGS

response to withdrawal symptoms

Heavy prolonged use of a drug can result in decreased satisfaction and increased tolerance to drug use. The withdrawal leads to increased discomfort, this results in cravings which take the form of "I need to use to feel well again", or the need or desire to take the drug to stop turkeying.

response to lack of pleasure

If to start with drugs were used to deal with unpleasant thoughts and feelings or to try to blot out bad memories, using is seen as the quickest, most extreme method of getting or keeping the good feelings.

conditioned craving

People are conditioned or learn to link certain normally innocent places or situations with drug use, e.g. car parks, streets, time of day, all of which can result in craving when drug free.

response to the desire for pleasure

People often get cravings when they want to heighten a pleasurable social experience, e.g. going out to the pub or clubbing.

MY PLAN TO CHANGE

So what you need now is your plan, no general worth his salt ever went into battle without a plan and you'd better believe, this is going to be a battle.

Spend time to think carefully. Get your support worker to help you work through and develop a realistic plan that sets out achievable short-term goals. Remember,

ONE STEP AT A TIME
Rome wasn't built in a day

Before you start, some basic thoughts on planning:

- **Everyone who has achieved anything had a plan**
- **Having a direction helps you get there**
- **Lack of organisation leads to chaos**
- **Planning organises chaos and leads to:**

    A sense of achievement

    The ability to cope

    Less stress

    The satisfaction at reaching one's goals

But remember, plans can be altered and modified, they are not written in stone.

SET SMALL ACHIEVABLE GOALS
REWARD YOURSELF WHEN YOU REACH THEM

Use the following format and fill in your own personal plan:

Date

The most important reasons why I want to change are:

My main goals for changing are:

I plan to do these things in order to reach my goal:

What?   When?

The first steps that I plan to take towards change are:
(Some things to consider are maybe, getting help with housing, relationships, illness or pain, things that make your drug use worse)

Other people who could help me in changing are:
(Look at who can give you support, doctor, drug worker, family member, or a friend)

Who?   **How could they help me?**

I hope with this plan to achieve these positive results:

My short-term goals are:
(Think very short term, e.g. tomorrow or next week)

My medium-term goals are:

My long-term goals are:
(Where would you like to be in the future?)

OBSTACLES TO SUCCESS

irrational thoughts
generalisation/rationalisation

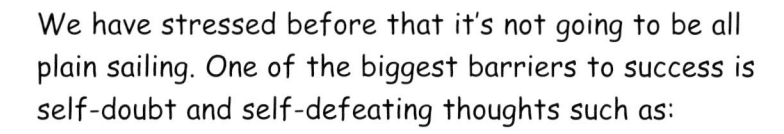

We have stressed before that it's not going to be all plain sailing. One of the biggest barriers to success is self-doubt and self-defeating thoughts such as:

"Once a junkie always a junkie"
If you believe that you believe anything

"I can't socialise without it"
Why not? Lots of other people manage to

"I can't cope without it"
You can learn other coping strategies

"I can't be normal without anything"
What's normal?

"I like the buzz, the rush"
Is it worth it? Are you still getting the same rush as when you started, or are you just using to stay normal?

"I'm sick, it's a disease"
Addiction is a choice, *your* choice

"Who gives a shit anyway?"
Lots of people do if you stand back and look

"Nobody cares about me"
Lots of people care about you

"All my old friends ignore me"
Are they still using?

and on and on and on ....

SKILLS NEEDED TO MAINTAIN THE CHANGE

To maintain the change you may need to learn new skills and relearn others. You will be able to work on some of these yourself. For others you will need the help of doctors, health workers, drug workers, etc. Some colleges run useful courses; check out what's available through your local library and by asking people who are supporting you to help with the search.

Look at the list and add some of your own to it:

Ability to say "NO"	Assertiveness skills
Stress management	Relaxation techniques
Time management skills	Goal setting
Positive thinking	Anger management

What other activities/skills can you add to the list?

Weighing up the PROS & CONS

Now you're a bit further on, let's look again at the pros and cons of giving up, add your own ideas to the list

GAINS	LOSSES
healthier lifestyle	friends, social life
no "legal" problems	buzz, excitement
extra money	ill health
self-esteem	
self-control	

STAYING CLEAN

Overcoming the boredom

Being addicted to drugs takes up a big chunk of your life and one of the difficulties of coming off is filling this void.

Think about the things that interest you and that you could do. You might not feel like signing up for a fulltime college course, but why not do something one night a week, just for fun.

You might not be able to afford a season ticket to Man United (or want, to, depending on your persuasion) but there are lots of local teams, some which you can watch for free.

The local library is a mine of information about clubs and activities. Look around your local area, check local papers for activities that are free.

There are lots of organisations looking for volunteers.

Depending on your age, there are organisations set up to provide activities for young people. They are keen to include as many people as possible on their courses, so where possible, some will stretch the age limits.

Use the ingenuity and resources you employed to find drugs to research your local areas for activities, courses and opportunities that interest you.

Part of "Supporting People" means that projects are now required to initiate "Meaningful Activities" for their clients so ask key workers, drug workers etc., where these can be found in your area.

Staying clean – the memories

Many people would argue that addiction is more mental than physical. If you think about it, it doesn't take long for any drug to come out of your system. Then what you are left with are the memories of using. What it was like, the buzz! Some users say that they can't imagine what they would do with their life if they gave up. This is why, it's important to take one day at a time.

Stimulants affect the balance of chemicals in the brain, mostly the ones that make us feel good and happy. It's possible, depending on the amount and length of time that you have used, that you may feel depressed and low. If this persists and you find it difficult to deal with, you should seek medical advice.

If it's too much to contemplate, don't plan to give up forever.

Just plan to give up for today.

Each day, tell yourself, "It's just for today".

Personal "Self Plan"

	I Would Like	Step One	Step Two	Step Three
Relationship				
Use of Time				
Housing				
Employment				
Money				
Drug Use				
Anything that is relevant to your personal situation				

Remember that the "Self Plan" is personal. Take manageable steps, at your own pace, one step at a time. If you plan properly, there's nothing that you can't achieve!
You can take control of your life if you want to, these tools can help you, they are not the answer, YOU ARE!

CERTIFICATE OF ATTENDANCE

This certificate is awarded to

_____

For completing the Personal Development Course

"Dealing with Crack—Cocaine Addiction"

_____
Date

_____
Signature
Facilitator

Crack Cocaine Quiz Answers

1 **False** It is not advisable for people with heart problems to use any stimulant drugs. High blood pressure, irregular heart contractions, chest pains, poorly oxygenated blood (greyness of the skin) are all symptoms of crack or cocaine abuse of the cardiovascular system.

2 **True** Damage to the brain by smoking crack or using cocaine is mainly caused by a stroke resulting from increased blood pressure due to the increased heart rate and the shrinking of the blood vessels, this decreases the blood supply to the brain.

3 **False** The problems caused by crack and cocaine on the lungs are commonly called "crack lung". This is due to the build up of fluid on the lungs, this produces symptoms very similar to asthma.

4 **False** Various reports have suggested that tuberculosis is on the increase. There is an increased risk of catching it if someone is smoking crack, particularly in a crack house, or is homeless, or if HIV positive. However, symptoms can be confused with general problems associated with crack/cocaine use.

5 **True** When using, the skin may become tender and sensitive. Lack of oxygen in the blood and an immune system impaired by continual use and in some cases the lack of personal hygiene, may cause skin conditions.

6 **False** Crack and cocaine can sometimes cause a drug-induced psychosis, particularly if use is high.

7 **True** Use can cause all of these things. It will also increase the amount of attacks that users have in conditions like Epilepsy and Sickle Cell.

8 **False** If injecting, the risks as the same as with injecting any other drug.

9 **False** Doctors do not have to report crack use to the Home Office.

10 **False** The sensation of "Coke Bug" is caused by the effects of crack or cocaine on the nerve endings.

11 **False** Overdose is possible – see page 16.